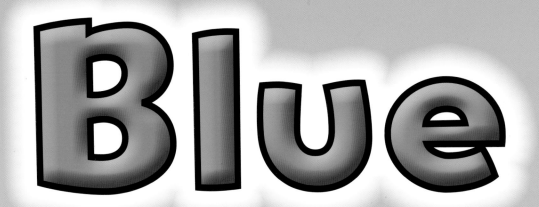

Blue

Rebecca Rissman

Raintree

www.raintreepublishers.co.uk
Visit our website to find out more information about Raintree books.

To order:
☎ Phone 0845 6044371
🖷 Fax +44 (0) 1865 312263
🖳 Email myorders@raintreepublishers.co.uk

Customers from outside the UK please telephone +44 1865 312262

Raintree is an imprint of Capstone Global Library Limited, a company incorporated in England and Wales having its registered office at 7 Pilgrim Street, London, EC4V 6LB – Registered company number: 6695582

Text © Capstone Global Library Limited 2012
First published in hardback in 2012
The moral rights of the proprietor have been asserted.

Edited by Dan Nunn, Rebecca Rissman, and Catherine Veitch
Designed by Joanna Hinton-Malivoire
Picture research by Elizabeth Alexander
Originated by Capstone Global Library Ltd.
Production by Victoria Fitzgerald
Printed in China by South China Printing Company Ltd

ISBN 978 1 406 22596 9
15 14 13 12 11
10 9 8 7 6 5 4 3 2 1

British Library Cataloguing in Publication Data
Rissman, Rebecca.
Blue. – (Colours All Around Us)
535.6-dc22

Acknowledgements
We would like to thank the following for permission to reproduce photographs: iStockphoto pp. 16 (© David Safanda), 21 (© Doug Schneider); Shutterstock pp. 4 (© Monkey Business Images), 5 (© Chamille White, © Veyron, © Maksim Toome, © Aksenova Natalya, © gregg Williams, © Paul Merrett), 7 (© Joerg Beuge), 9 (© Sari ONeal), 11 (© matka_Wariatka), 13 (© H&B), 15 (© Natalia Dobryanskaya), 17 (© marrio31), 19 (© BlueOrange Studio), 22 left (© Olinchuk), 22 right (© Ruth Black), 23 top left (© Tatiana Popova), 23 top right (© Rufous), 23 bottom left (© Nordling), 23 bottom right (© vilax).

Front cover photograph of a shoal of fish reproduced with permission of Shutterstock (© Rich Carey). Back cover photographs reproduced with permission of Shutterstock (© Ruth Black, © Aksenova Natalya, © Veyron, © Nordling).

Contents

Blue all around us

Let's look for colours.
It's time to play!

How many blue things
can you find today?

Good morning!

It's breakfast time!
What do you want to eat?

Blueberries in your bowl!
What a tasty treat!

yum, yum!

Out of the window!

Can you see the butterfly?
It's flying by outside.

It has landed on a flower,
And spread its wings out wide!

Take a walk

Let's go for a walk. The sun is bright. Wear a blue hat to block out the light!

Look up!

Look in the sky!
There's a bird flying past!

Its feathers are blue.
It's flying so **fast**!

Dive in!

Let's go to the beach.
Do you like to swim?

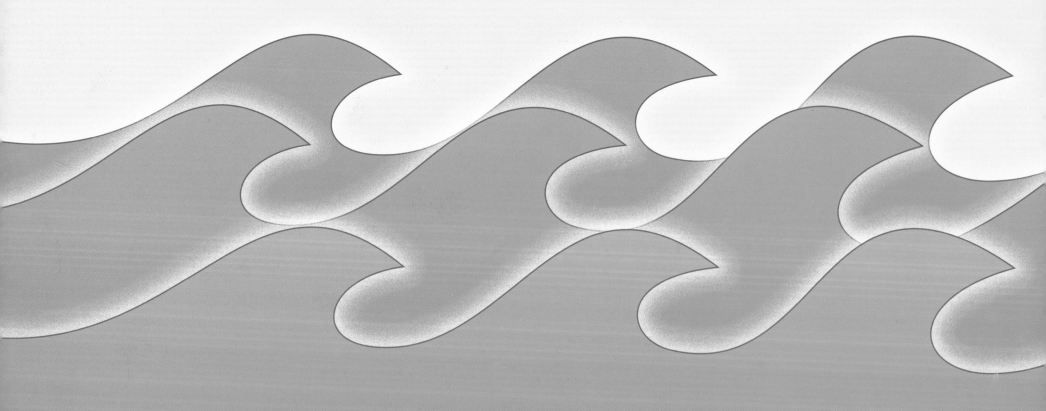

The sea is blue.
Time to jump in!

Blue fish

Look in the water.
Are blue fish nearby?

bubble,
bubble

Oh, aren't you clever?
You found them first try!

Sailing fun

Do you want to go sailing?
Let's sail out west.

Which boat should we take?
The blue boat is best!

Heading home

It's been a long day.
The sun is getting low.

The blue watch on your wrist says it's time to go!

21

What else is blue?

What a day for colours!
Blue things are everywhere.

Can you make a list?

23

Colour challenge

Can you find two blue butterflies in this book?

Index